Daily Planner

Date: _____

GOALS
How can your team best support you today?

-
-
-

How much water have you had today?

TO-DO-LIST
Check off your tasks throughout the day.

-
-
-

When was the last time you checked your blood pressure? Record below.

WHAT IS THE BEST PART OF YOUR DAY?

_____
_____
_____
_____
_____

Memo

Daily Planner

Date: _____

GOALS
How can your team best support you today?

-
-
-

How much water have you had today?

TO-DO-LIST
Check off your tasks throughout the day.

-
-
-

When was the last time you checked your blood pressure? Record below.

WHAT IS THE BEST PART OF YOUR DAY?

_____
_____
_____
_____
_____

Memo

Daily Planner

Date: _____

GOALS
How can your team best support you today?

-
-
-

How much water have you had today?

TO-DO-LIST
Check off your tasks throughout the day.

-
-
-

When was the last time you checked your blood pressure? Record below.

WHAT IS THE BEST PART OF YOUR DAY?

_____
_____
_____
_____
_____

Memo

Daily Planner

Date: _____

GOALS
How can your team best support you today?

-
-
-

How much water have you had today?

TO-DO-LIST
Check off your tasks throughout the day.

-
-
-

When was the last time you checked your blood pressure? Record below.

WHAT IS THE BEST PART OF YOUR DAY?

_____
_____
_____
_____
_____

Memo

Daily Planner

Date: _____

GOALS
How can your team best support you today?

-
-
-

How much water have you had today?

TO-DO-LIST
Check off your tasks throughout the day.

-
-
-

When was the last time you checked your blood pressure? Record below.

WHAT IS THE BEST PART OF YOUR DAY?

_____
_____
_____
_____
_____

Memo

Daily Planner

Date: _____

GOALS
How can your team best support you today?

-
-
-

How much water have you had today?

TO-DO-LIST
Check off your tasks throughout the day.

-
-
-

When was the last time you checked your blood pressure? Record below.

WHAT IS THE BEST PART OF YOUR DAY?

_____
_____
_____
_____

Memo

Daily Planner

Date: _____

GOALS

How can your team best support you today?

-
-
-

How much water have you had today?

TO-DO-LIST

Check off your tasks throughout the day.

-
-
-

When was the last time you checked your blood pressure? Record below.

WHAT IS THE BEST PART OF YOUR DAY?

_____
_____
_____
_____

Memo

Daily Planner

Date: _____

GOALS

How can your team best support you today?

-
-
-

How much water have you had today?

TO-DO-LIST

Check off your tasks throughout the day.

-
-
-

When was the last time you checked your blood pressure? Record below.

WHAT IS THE BEST PART OF YOUR DAY?

_____
_____
_____
_____
_____

Memo

Daily Planner

Date: _____

GOALS

How can your team best support you today?

-
-
-

How much water have you had today?

TO-DO-LIST

Check off your tasks throughout the day.

-
-
-

When was the last time you checked your blood pressure? Record below.

WHAT IS THE BEST PART OF YOUR DAY?

_____
_____
_____
_____
_____

Memo

Daily Planner

Date: _____

GOALS

How can your team best support you today?

-
-
-

How much water have you had today?

TO-DO-LIST

Check off your tasks throughout the day.

-
-
-

When was the last time you checked your blood pressure? Record below.

WHAT IS THE BEST PART OF YOUR DAY?

_____
_____
_____
_____

Memo

Daily Planner

Date: _____

GOALS

How can your team best support you today?

-
-
-

How much water have you had today?

TO-DO-LIST

Check off your tasks throughout the day.

-
-
-

When was the last time you checked your blood pressure? Record below.

WHAT IS THE BEST PART OF YOUR DAY?

_____
_____
_____
_____
_____

Memo

Daily Planner

Date: _____

GOALS

How can your team best support you today?

-
-
-

How much water have you had today?

TO-DO-LIST

Check off your tasks throughout the day.

-
-
-

When was the last time you checked your blood pressure? Record below.

WHAT IS THE BEST PART OF YOUR DAY?

_____
_____
_____
_____
_____

Memo

Daily Planner

Date: _____

GOALS
How can your team best support you today?

-
-
-

How much water have you had today?

TO-DO-LIST
Check off your tasks throughout the day.

- [ ]
- [ ]
- [ ]

When was the last time you checked your blood pressure? Record below.

WHAT IS THE BEST PART OF YOUR DAY?

_____
_____
_____
_____
_____

Memo

Daily Planner

Date: _____

GOALS
How can your team best support you today?

-
-
-

How much water have you had today?

TO-DO-LIST
Check off your tasks throughout the day.

- [ ]
- [ ]
- [ ]

When was the last time you checked your blood pressure? Record below.

WHAT IS THE BEST PART OF YOUR DAY?

_____
_____
_____
_____
_____

Memo

Daily Planner

Date: _____

GOALS

How can your team best support you today?

-
-
-

How much water have you had today?

TO-DO-LIST

Check off your tasks throughout the day.

-
-
-

When was the last time you checked your blood pressure? Record below.

WHAT IS THE BEST PART OF YOUR DAY?

_____
_____
_____
_____
_____

Memo

Daily Planner

Date: _____

GOALS

How can your team best support you today?

-
-
-

How much water have you had today?

TO-DO-LIST

Check off your tasks throughout the day.

-
-
-

When was the last time you checked your blood pressure? Record below.

WHAT IS THE BEST PART OF YOUR DAY?

_____
_____
_____
_____
_____

Memo

Daily Planner

Date: _____

GOALS

How can your team best support you today?

-
-
-

How much water have you had today?

TO-DO-LIST

Check off your tasks throughout the day.

-
-
-

When was the last time you checked your blood pressure? Record below.

WHAT IS THE BEST PART OF YOUR DAY?

_____
_____
_____
_____
_____

Memo

Daily Planner

Date: _____

GOALS

How can your team best support you today?

-
-
-

How much water have you had today?

TO-DO-LIST

Check off your tasks throughout the day.

-
-
-

When was the last time you checked your blood pressure? Record below.

WHAT IS THE BEST PART OF YOUR DAY?

_____
_____
_____
_____
_____

Memo

Daily Planner

Date: _____

GOALS

How can your team best support you today?

-
-
-

How much water have you had today?

TO-DO-LIST

Check off your tasks throughout the day.

-
-
-

When was the last time you checked your blood pressure? Record below.

WHAT IS THE BEST PART OF YOUR DAY?

_____
_____
_____
_____
_____

Memo

Daily Planner

Date: _____

GOALS

How can your team best support you today?

-
-
-

How much water have you had today?

TO-DO-LIST

Check off your tasks throughout the day.

-
-
-

When was the last time you checked your blood pressure? Record below.

WHAT IS THE BEST PART OF YOUR DAY?

_____
_____
_____
_____
_____

Memo

Daily Planner

Date: _____

GOALS
How can your team best support you today?

-
-
-

How much water have you had today?

TO-DO-LIST
Check off your tasks throughout the day.

-
-
-

When was the last time you checked your blood pressure? Record below.

WHAT IS THE BEST PART OF YOUR DAY?

_____
_____
_____
_____
_____

Memo

Daily Planner

Date: _____

GOALS
How can your team best support you today?

-
-
-

How much water have you had today?

TO-DO-LIST
Check off your tasks throughout the day.

-
-
-

When was the last time you checked your blood pressure? Record below.

WHAT IS THE BEST PART OF YOUR DAY?

_____
_____
_____
_____
_____

Memo

Daily Planner

Date: _____

GOALS

How can your team best support you today?

-
-
-

How much water have you had today?

TO-DO-LIST

Check off your tasks throughout the day.

-
-
-

When was the last time you checked your blood pressure? Record below.

WHAT IS THE BEST PART OF YOUR DAY?

_____
_____
_____
_____
_____

Memo

Daily Planner

Date: _____

GOALS

How can your team best support you today?

-
-
-

How much water have you had today?

TO-DO-LIST

Check off your tasks throughout the day.

-
-
-

When was the last time you checked your blood pressure? Record below.

WHAT IS THE BEST PART OF YOUR DAY?

_____
_____
_____
_____
_____

Memo

Daily Planner

Date: _____

GOALS
How can your team best support you today?

-
-
-

How much water have you had today?

TO-DO-LIST
Check off your tasks throughout the day.

-
-
-

When was the last time you checked your blood pressure? Record below.

WHAT IS THE BEST PART OF YOUR DAY?

_____
_____
_____
_____
_____

Memo

Daily Planner

Date: _____

GOALS

How can your team best support you today?

-
-
-

How much water have you had today?

TO-DO-LIST

Check off your tasks throughout the day.

-
-
-

When was the last time you checked your blood pressure? Record below.

WHAT IS THE BEST PART OF YOUR DAY?

_____
_____
_____
_____
_____

Memo

Daily Planner

Date: _____

GOALS

How can your team best support you today?

- ■
- ■
- ■

How much water have you had today?

TO-DO-LIST

Check off your tasks throughout the day.

- ■
- ■
- ■

When was the last time you checked your blood pressure? Record below.

WHAT IS THE BEST PART OF YOUR DAY?

_____
_____
_____
_____
_____

Memo

Daily Planner

Date: _____

GOALS

How can your team best support you today?

- ■
- ■
- ■

How much water have you had today?

TO-DO-LIST

Check off your tasks throughout the day.

- ■
- ■
- ■

When was the last time you checked your blood pressure? Record below.

WHAT IS THE BEST PART OF YOUR DAY?

_____
_____
_____
_____
_____
_____

Memo

Daily Planner

Date: _____

GOALS
How can your team best support you today?

- ▪
- ▪
- ▪

How much water have you had today?

TO-DO-LIST
Check off your tasks throughout the day.

- ▪
- ▪
- ▪

When was the last time you checked your blood pressure? Record below.

WHAT IS THE BEST PART OF YOUR DAY?

_____
_____
_____
_____
_____

Memo

Daily Planner

Date: _____

GOALS
How can your team best support you today?

-
-
-

How much water have you had today?

TO-DO-LIST
Check off your tasks throughout the day.

-
-
-

When was the last time you checked your blood pressure? Record below.

WHAT IS THE BEST PART OF YOUR DAY?

_____
_____
_____
_____
_____

Memo

Daily Planner

Date: _____

GOALS

How can your team best support you today?

- ▪
- ▪
- ▪

How much water have you had today?

TO-DO-LIST

Check off your tasks throughout the day.

- ▪
- ▪
- ▪

When was the last time you checked your blood pressure? Record below.

WHAT IS THE BEST PART OF YOUR DAY?

_____
_____
_____
_____
_____

Memo

Daily Planner

Date: _____

GOALS

How can your team best support you today?

-
-
-

How much water have you had today?

TO-DO-LIST

Check off your tasks throughout the day.

-
-
-

When was the last time you checked your blood pressure? Record below.

WHAT IS THE BEST PART OF YOUR DAY?

_____
_____
_____
_____
_____

Memo

Daily Planner

Date: _____

GOALS
How can your team best support you today?

- ▪
- ▪
- ▪

How much water have you had today?

TO-DO-LIST
Check off your tasks throughout the day.

- ▪
- ▪
- ▪

When was the last time you checked your blood pressure? Record below.

WHAT IS THE BEST PART OF YOUR DAY?

_____
_____
_____
_____
_____

Memo

Daily Planner

Date: _____

GOALS
How can your team best support you today?

-
-
-

How much water have you had today?

TO-DO-LIST
Check off your tasks throughout the day.

-
-
-

When was the last time you checked your blood pressure? Record below.

WHAT IS THE BEST PART OF YOUR DAY?

_____
_____
_____
_____
_____

Memo

Daily Planner

Date: _____

GOALS
How can your team best support you today?

-
-
-

How much water have you had today?

TO-DO-LIST
Check off your tasks throughout the day.

-
-
-

When was the last time you checked your blood pressure? Record below.

WHAT IS THE BEST PART OF YOUR DAY?

_____
_____
_____
_____
_____

Memo

Daily Planner

Date: _____

GOALS
How can your team best support you today?

- ■
- ■
- ■

How much water have you had today?

TO-DO-LIST
Check off your tasks throughout the day.

- ■
- ■
- ■

When was the last time you checked your blood pressure? Record below.

WHAT IS THE BEST PART OF YOUR DAY?

_____
_____
_____
_____
_____

Memo

Daily Planner

Date: _____

GOALS

How can your team best support you today?

-
-
-

How much water have you had today?

TO-DO-LIST

Check off your tasks throughout the day.

-
-
-

When was the last time you checked your blood pressure? Record below.

WHAT IS THE BEST PART OF YOUR DAY?

_____
_____
_____
_____
_____

Memo

Daily Planner

Date: _____

GOALS
How can your team best support you today?

-
-
-

How much water have you had today?

TO-DO-LIST
Check off your tasks throughout the day.

-
-
-

When was the last time you checked your blood pressure? Record below.

WHAT IS THE BEST PART OF YOUR DAY?

_____
_____
_____
_____
_____

Memo

Daily Planner

Date: _____

GOALS
How can your team best support you today?

-
-
-

How much water have you had today?

TO-DO-LIST
Check off your tasks throughout the day.

-
-
-

When was the last time you checked your blood pressure? Record below.

WHAT IS THE BEST PART OF YOUR DAY?

_____
_____
_____
_____
_____
_____

Memo

Daily Planner

Date: _____

GOALS
How can your team best support you today?

-
-
-

How much water have you had today?

TO-DO-LIST
Check off your tasks throughout the day.

-
-
-

When was the last time you checked your blood pressure? Record below.

WHAT IS THE BEST PART OF YOUR DAY?

_____
_____
_____
_____
_____

Memo

Daily Planner

Date: _____

GOALS

How can your team best support you today?

-
-
-

How much water have you had today?

TO-DO-LIST

Check off your tasks throughout the day.

-
-
-

When was the last time you checked your blood pressure? Record below.

WHAT IS THE BEST PART OF YOUR DAY?

_____
_____
_____
_____
_____

Memo

Daily Planner

Date: _____

GOALS

How can your team best support you today?

- ▪
- ▪
- ▪

How much water have you had today?

TO-DO-LIST

Check off your tasks throughout the day.

- ▪
- ▪
- ▪

When was the last time you checked your blood pressure? Record below.

WHAT IS THE BEST PART OF YOUR DAY?

_____
_____
_____
_____
_____

Memo

Daily Planner

Date: _____

GOALS

How can your team best support you today?

-
-
-

How much water have you had today?

TO-DO-LIST

Check off your tasks throughout the day.

-
-
-

When was the last time you checked your blood pressure? Record below.

WHAT IS THE BEST PART OF YOUR DAY?

_____
_____
_____
_____
_____

Memo

Daily Planner

Date: _____

GOALS
How can your team best support you today?

-
-
-

How much water have you had today?

TO-DO-LIST
Check off your tasks throughout the day.

-
-
-

When was the last time you checked your blood pressure? Record below.

WHAT IS THE BEST PART OF YOUR DAY?

_____
_____
_____
_____
_____

Memo

Daily Planner

Date: _____

GOALS

How can your team best support you today?

-
-
-

How much water have you had today?

TO-DO-LIST

Check off your tasks throughout the day.

-
-
-

When was the last time you checked your blood pressure? Record below.

WHAT IS THE BEST PART OF YOUR DAY?

_____
_____
_____
_____
_____
_____

Memo

Daily Planner

Date: _____

GOALS
How can your team best support you today?

-
-
-

How much water have you had today?

TO-DO-LIST
Check off your tasks throughout the day.

-
-
-

When was the last time you checked your blood pressure? Record below.

WHAT IS THE BEST PART OF YOUR DAY?

_____
_____
_____
_____
_____

Memo

Daily Planner

Date: _____

GOALS

How can your team best support you today?

-
-
-

How much water have you had today?

TO-DO-LIST

Check off your tasks throughout the day.

-
-
-

When was the last time you checked your blood pressure? Record below.

WHAT IS THE BEST PART OF YOUR DAY?

_____
_____
_____
_____
_____

Memo

Daily Planner

Date: _____

GOALS
How can your team best support you today?

-
-
-

How much water have you had today?

TO-DO-LIST
Check off your tasks throughout the day.

-
-
-

When was the last time you checked your blood pressure? Record below.

WHAT IS THE BEST PART OF YOUR DAY?

_____
_____
_____
_____
_____

Memo

Daily Planner

Date: _____

GOALS
How can your team best support you today?

-
-
-

How much water have you had today?

TO-DO-LIST
Check off your tasks throughout the day.

-
-
-

When was the last time you checked your blood pressure? Record below.

WHAT IS THE BEST PART OF YOUR DAY?

_____
_____
_____
_____
_____
_____

Memo

Daily Planner

Date: _____

GOALS

How can your team best support you today?

-
-
-

How much water have you had today?

TO-DO-LIST

Check off your tasks throughout the day.

-
-
-

When was the last time you checked your blood pressure? Record below.

WHAT IS THE BEST PART OF YOUR DAY?

_____
_____
_____
_____
_____

Memo

Daily Planner

Date: _____

GOALS
How can your team best support you today?

-
-
-

How much water have you had today?

TO-DO-LIST
Check off your tasks throughout the day.

-
-
-

When was the last time you checked your blood pressure? Record below.

WHAT IS THE BEST PART OF YOUR DAY?

_____
_____
_____
_____
_____

Memo

Daily Planner

Date: _____

GOALS

How can your team best support you today?

-
-
-

How much water have you had today?

TO-DO-LIST

Check off your tasks throughout the day.

-
-
-

When was the last time you checked your blood pressure? Record below.

WHAT IS THE BEST PART OF YOUR DAY?

_____
_____
_____
_____
_____

Memo

Daily Planner

Date: _____

GOALS

How can your team best support you today?

-
-
-

How much water have you had today?

TO-DO-LIST

Check off your tasks throughout the day.

-
-
-

When was the last time you checked your blood pressure? Record below.

WHAT IS THE BEST PART OF YOUR DAY?

_____
_____
_____
_____
_____

Memo

Daily Planner

Date: _____

GOALS

How can your team best support you today?

-
-
-

How much water have you had today?

TO-DO-LIST

Check off your tasks throughout the day.

-
-
-

When was the last time you checked your blood pressure? Record below.

WHAT IS THE BEST PART OF YOUR DAY?

_____
_____
_____
_____
_____

Memo

Daily Planner

Date: _____

GOALS
How can your team best support you today?

-
-
-

How much water have you had today?

TO-DO-LIST
Check off your tasks throughout the day.

-
-
-

When was the last time you checked your blood pressure? Record below.

WHAT IS THE BEST PART OF YOUR DAY?

_____
_____
_____
_____
_____

Memo

Daily Planner

Date: _____

GOALS
How can your team best support you today?

-
-
-

How much water have you had today?

TO-DO-LIST
Check off your tasks throughout the day.

-
-
-

When was the last time you checked your blood pressure? Record below.

WHAT IS THE BEST PART OF YOUR DAY?

_____
_____
_____
_____
_____

Memo

Daily Planner

Date: _____

GOALS

How can your team best support you today?

-
-
-

How much water have you had today?

TO-DO-LIST

Check off your tasks throughout the day.

-
-
-

When was the last time you checked your blood pressure? Record below.

WHAT IS THE BEST PART OF YOUR DAY?

_____
_____
_____
_____
_____

Memo

Daily Planner

Date: _____

GOALS
How can your team best support you today?

-
-
-

How much water have you had today?

TO-DO-LIST
Check off your tasks throughout the day.

-
-
-

When was the last time you checked your blood pressure? Record below.

WHAT IS THE BEST PART OF YOUR DAY?

_____
_____
_____
_____
_____

Memo

Daily Planner

Date: _____

GOALS
How can your team best support you today?

- ◼
- ◼
- ◼

How much water have you had today?

TO-DO-LIST
Check off your tasks throughout the day.

- ◼
- ◼
- ◼

When was the last time you checked your blood pressure? Record below.

WHAT IS THE BEST PART OF YOUR DAY?

_____
_____
_____
_____
_____

Memo

Daily Planner

Date: _____

GOALS
How can your team best support you today?

- ■
- ■
- ■

How much water have you had today?

TO-DO-LIST
Check off your tasks throughout the day.

- ■
- ■
- ■

When was the last time you checked your blood pressure? Record below.

WHAT IS THE BEST PART OF YOUR DAY?

_____
_____
_____
_____
_____

Memo

Daily Planner

Date: _____

GOALS

How can your team best support you today?

-
-
-

How much water have you had today?

TO-DO-LIST

Check off your tasks throughout the day.

-
-
-

When was the last time you checked your blood pressure? Record below.

WHAT IS THE BEST PART OF YOUR DAY?

_____
_____
_____
_____
_____

Memo

Daily Planner

Date: _____

GOALS
How can your team best support you today?

-
-
-

How much water have you had today?

TO-DO-LIST
Check off your tasks throughout the day.

-
-
-

When was the last time you checked your blood pressure? Record below.

WHAT IS THE BEST PART OF YOUR DAY?

_____
_____
_____
_____
_____

Memo

Daily Planner

Date: _____

GOALS

How can your team best support you today?

-
-
-

How much water have you had today?

TO-DO-LIST

Check off your tasks throughout the day.

-
-
-

When was the last time you checked your blood pressure? Record below.

WHAT IS THE BEST PART OF YOUR DAY?

_____
_____
_____
_____
_____

Memo

Daily Planner

Date: _____

GOALS
How can your team best support you today?

-
-
-

How much water have you had today?

TO-DO-LIST
Check off your tasks throughout the day.

-
-
-

When was the last time you checked your blood pressure? Record below.

WHAT IS THE BEST PART OF YOUR DAY?

_____
_____
_____
_____
_____

Memo

Daily Planner

Date: _____

GOALS
How can your team best support you today?

-
-
-

How much water have you had today?

TO-DO-LIST
Check off your tasks throughout the day.

-
-
-

When was the last time you checked your blood pressure? Record below.

WHAT IS THE BEST PART OF YOUR DAY?

_____
_____
_____
_____
_____

Memo

Daily Planner

Date: _____

GOALS
How can your team best support you today?

-
-
-

How much water have you had today?

TO-DO-LIST
Check off your tasks throughout the day.

-
-
-

When was the last time you checked your blood pressure? Record below.

WHAT IS THE BEST PART OF YOUR DAY?

_____
_____
_____
_____
_____

Memo

Daily Planner

Date: _____

GOALS

How can your team best support you today?

-
-
-

How much water have you had today?

TO-DO-LIST

Check off your tasks throughout the day.

-
-
-

When was the last time you checked your blood pressure? Record below.

WHAT IS THE BEST PART OF YOUR DAY?

_____
_____
_____
_____
_____
_____

Memo

Daily Planner

Date: _____

GOALS

How can your team best support you today?

-
-
-

How much water have you had today?

TO-DO-LIST

Check off your tasks throughout the day.

-
-
-

When was the last time you checked your blood pressure? Record below.

WHAT IS THE BEST PART OF YOUR DAY?

_____
_____
_____
_____
_____

Memo

Daily Planner

Date: _____

GOALS
How can your team best support you today?

-
-
-

How much water have you had today?

TO-DO-LIST
Check off your tasks throughout the day.

-
-
-

When was the last time you checked your blood pressure? Record below.

WHAT IS THE BEST PART OF YOUR DAY?

_____
_____
_____
_____
_____

Memo

Daily Planner

Date: _____

GOALS
How can your team best support you today?

-
-
-

How much water have you had today?

TO-DO-LIST
Check off your tasks throughout the day.

-
-
-

When was the last time you checked your blood pressure? Record below.

WHAT IS THE BEST PART OF YOUR DAY?

_____
_____
_____
_____
_____
_____

Memo

Daily Planner

Date: _____

GOALS
How can your team best support you today?

-
-
-

How much water have you had today?

TO-DO-LIST
Check off your tasks throughout the day.

-
-
-

When was the last time you checked your blood pressure? Record below.

WHAT IS THE BEST PART OF YOUR DAY?

_____
_____
_____
_____
_____
_____

Memo

Daily Planner

Date: _____

GOALS

How can your team best support you today?

-
-
-

How much water have you had today?

TO-DO-LIST

Check off your tasks throughout the day.

-
-
-

When was the last time you checked your blood pressure? Record below.

WHAT IS THE BEST PART OF YOUR DAY?

_____
_____
_____
_____
_____

Memo

Daily Planner

Date: _____

GOALS
How can your team best support you today?

■

■

■

How much water have you had today?

TO-DO-LIST
Check off your tasks throughout the day.

■

■

■

When was the last time you checked your blood pressure? Record below.

WHAT IS THE BEST PART OF YOUR DAY?

_____
_____
_____
_____
_____

Memo

Daily Planner

Date: _____

GOALS

How can your team best support you today?

-
-
-

How much water have you had today?

TO-DO-LIST

Check off your tasks throughout the day.

-
-
-

When was the last time you checked your blood pressure? Record below.

WHAT IS THE BEST PART OF YOUR DAY?

_____
_____
_____
_____
_____

Memo

Daily Planner

Date: _____

GOALS
How can your team best support you today?

-
-
-

How much water have you had today?

TO-DO-LIST
Check off your tasks throughout the day.

-
-
-

When was the last time you checked your blood pressure? Record below.

WHAT IS THE BEST PART OF YOUR DAY?

_____
_____
_____
_____
_____

Memo

www.ingramcontent.com/pod-product-compliance
Lightning Source LLC
LaVergne TN
LVHW070539070526
838199LV00076B/6806